Contents

English

Maths

By Sam Lovegrove

Foreword

There is a whole world to be explored outside the classroom. Children spend quite a lot of time – I seem to remember from my teaching days and my own school days before that – just gazing through the window, longing to be out there. Of course, there is the natural longing to play outside, to run free, to have fun outdoors – and that is important, a vital part of growing up.

But, for teachers and children, that outdoor world can also be a great resource for learning – learning about nature and wildlife, about growing our food, about caring for our world, about taking responsibility for its conservation. And then there is also the kind of learning that supports work in the classroom. Here again the outdoors can stimulate interest and enthusiasm, whether for maths or literacy or art or music. It can teach children to observe, opening their eyes and hearts and minds to new ways of learning.

The best way I ever discovered of encouraging children to write – which was my particular enthusiasm as a teacher, of course – was to go out with them, all of us with notebooks, to sit and watch, to talk about it for a while and then to write and sketch what we saw, what we heard and smelt and felt. Then we would draw that world in words or in pictures. It opened worlds for them – and for me too, as a teacher and as a writer.

Michael Morpurgo

Introduction

This book is designed to help you take your teaching outdoors and into the school grounds. Each of the 30 activities focuses on specific maths and English learning outcomes, with National Curriculum links, and aims to inspire you to deliver lessons outside the confines of the classroom.

The practical tasks outlined in the book support a variety of learning needs and cater for all learners. The activities can also be differentiated according to the needs of your own class to ensure that each pupil can achieve the learning objective.

The book offers the following opportunities for differentiation:

Content of the activity – The content can be adapted to enable individuals and groups to engage in the activities with varying degrees of support. Similarly, the suggested reading materials can be adapted or replaced with easier or more complex texts.

Grouping – Working in groups or with a partner helps pupils to access knowledge, increase their understanding, develop concepts and practise skills; it also enables self-assessment, cooperation and mutual support.

Working in mixed-ability groups allows lower achievers to take advantage of peer support, whilst higher achievers have the opportunity to organise and voice their thoughts and to gain experience of explaining concepts and ideas. Roles can be allocated within the group according to each pupil's skill set and learning needs.

Working in ability groups allows for specific targeting of content and for a group of pupils working at a similar level to be allocated appropriate resources and levels of support.

Environment – It is important to consider the physical environment and demands of some of the activities, particularly if pupils have specific physical or medical needs, for example placing equipment for ease of access or considering visibility for pupils with visual problems.

Resources – Differentiating resources will allow pupils to access the activities at their own level. Some pupils may require adaptations to texts. Using a wide range of materials can allow a single learning outcome to be achieved by the whole class. A tablet device can enable a dyslexic or physically impaired pupil to achieve the desired outcome.

Pace – Each activity is designed to be completed in an hour. However, if some less able pupils find it difficult to complete tasks within the allotted timescale, the activity may need to be adapted. The extension activities can be used to challenge more able pupils.

Dialogue and support – Differentiation by dialogue can help to identify which pupils need detailed explanations in simple language and which pupils can engage in dialogue at a more sophisticated level. Questioning can be targeted to produce a range of responses, challenging more able pupils and enabling verbal support and encouragement to be given where needed.

Outcomes – The outcomes of pupil learning should demonstrate understanding of the knowledge or concept taught or mastery of the skill. Differentiation by outcome enables all pupils to undertake the same open-ended activity, but allows pupils to arrive at a personalised outcome according to their level of ability. This is useful, particularly for written work, and is embedded into many of the activities.

Assessment – By observing and questioning pupils throughout the activities, the lessons can be continuously adjusted according to the learners' needs. End-of-lesson assessments can be adapted according to the abilities of individual pupils.

National Curriculum links

Reading – comprehension

- participate in discussion about books, poems and other works that are read to them and those that they can read for themselves, taking turns and listening to what others say

Writing – composition

- develop positive attitudes towards and stamina for writing by:
  - o writing narratives about personal experiences and those of others (real and fictional)

Vocabulary	illustration, compose, identify, motif, story starter, sentence
Resources	a copy of Leaf Man by Lois Ehlert; fallen leaves from a variety of tree and plant species; glue; tape; story paper (lined paper with space for a picture); pre-printed story starter sheets (first page: Leaf Man blew east/west/south/north (depending on the group), past the …; second page: Towards the …); pencils; clipboards; compass; leaf identification guide
Prior learning	imaginative writing, transcription and composition
Cross-curricular links	Geography – compass directions; Art – using materials creatively; Science – plant identification

Introduction

Read Leaf Man by Lois Ehlert, as a class. Discuss the journey Leaf Man goes on, and what takes him on the journey. Show the class the inside of the book and the illustrations that name the leaves. Discuss how the illustrations are all made from leaves, and talk about the different colours and sizes.

Tell the class they will be writing their own Leaf Man book. Ask them to think about what Leaf Man would see if he were travelling around their school.

Leaf Man leaves school

This activity is best done in early autumn. Ask the pupils to collect as many fallen leaves as they can, in all sizes and colours. Look at the leaves, and use the leaf identification guide to name some of them.

Show the pupils the compass, and mark north, south, east and west on the ground. Ask the pupils to see if they can feel any wind on their faces. If not, they could try wetting a finger, holding it up and seeing which side feels colder; that's where the wind is coming from. Give each pupil a leaf and, when the wind blows, even a little, ask them to hold their leaf up high then let it go and watch which way it goes.

Divide the pupils into four groups and give each pupil a pencil and some story paper. Ask one group to visit the north part of the school grounds, one the south, one the west and one the east, and to write or draw where their own Leaf Man could visit. Ask them to think about what is above the ground and below the ground, what he would see if he was flying in the wind, and how the school would look from the air. Look for areas in the school grounds that are similar to the areas in the book; for example, the school vegetable garden could be the pumpkin patch or the school field could be the marshes.

Explain that each pupil is going to create two pages of a class version of *Leaf Man*. Give each member of the group two sheets of story paper with the following story starters already printed on the page: 'Leaf Man blew east/west/south/north (*depending on the group*), past the … (write what you saw from 'flying in the wind')' and (*on the second page*) 'Towards the …'.

Give pupils 10 minutes to finish their sentences, and explain that they should choose what to write based on what they observed in their area earlier.

Provide glue and tape and give the pupils another 10 minutes to create a picture using their own drawings and sticking some leaves on their sheets to illustrate their sentences.

Come back together and discuss sentences from each group, comparing the differences from each area.

 Extension activity: Discuss interesting ideas for a further class story about Leaf Man. Use a flip chart and scribe the story for the pupils, asking them where to include the motif 'The Leaf Man has to go where the wind blows'. Include ideas from each group in the class story, and read the completed story together. Then look again at the collected leaves and, using a leaf identification guide, label each of them to display with the finished stories.

 Recording/evidencing: Use the pupils' written sentences and pictures to make a class collection to display in class.

 Assessment methods: Listen to the pupils as they take part in the discussions and as they contribute to the shared story; observe them as they take part in the activity, and record your observations. Assess their composed sentences, looking for their ability to create sentences and narrative based on the Leaf Man's journey.

Facts and fiction

National Curriculum links

Reading – comprehension

- participate in discussion about books, poems and other works that are read to them and those that they can read for themselves, taking turns and listening to what others say

- draw on what they already know or on background information and vocabulary provided by the teacher

- be introduced to non-fiction books that are structured in different ways

Writing – composition

- develop positive attitudes towards and stamina for writing by:
  - writing narratives about personal experiences and those of others (real and fictional)

Writing – vocabulary, grammar and punctuation

- learn how to use sentences with different forms: statement

Vocabulary	identification, imagination, fiction, non-fiction, sentence, statement
Resources	a copy of *Stanley's Stick* by John Hegley; sticks in differing sizes (some dead and some freshly cut); lined paper and pencils; twig identification guide; tree information books or fact sheets from the Woodland Trust
Prior learning	group discussion and debates
Cross-curricular links	Science – plant identification

Introduction

Read *Stanley's Stick* by John Hegley together and discuss the story. Ask pupils what they thought about the story, how Stanley felt about his stick, and if they have any toys that can be more than one thing. Talk about when they play outdoors and ask if, like Stanley, they like to play with sticks and what they like to do with them.

Discuss briefly how to play safely with sticks: small sticks should be carried, larger sticks should be dragged or carried with a classmate, and sticks should not be used for hitting.

When is a stick not a stick?

Explore any wooded area of the school grounds on a class stick hunt, explaining to the pupils to collect only fallen sticks – thin ones that they can easily break, and no longer than their forearm. Ideally, each pupil should have a stick. Model how a freshly cut stick is still bendy but a deadwood stick snaps. Ask the pupils what the snapping sounds like – can they hear a fire crackling? Ask what uses each stick could have (e.g. for woodworking or as a home to thousands of mini-beasts).

Model how to use a twig identification guide. Help pupils to identify which tree some of the sticks came from, and assist them with new vocabulary or with reading more difficult words. Show the pupils a tree information book or fact sheet and discuss how it is different from *Stanley's Stick*. Is the subject still the same? Read a statement from the information text and read a sentence from *Stanley's Stick*. Ask the pupils to identify which sentence is from the story (fiction) and which is a fact (non-fiction).

Explain to the pupils that they are going to write some facts and some fiction about their stick. Give each pupil a piece of lined paper and ask them to write answers to the following:

- What tree is the stick from? (e.g. 'My stick is from a birch tree.')

- Write a description of the stick. (e.g. 'It is light grey and peeling.')

- How do you feel about the stick? (e.g. 'It is brilliant and I love it.')

- What could it be? Explain that this is the fiction and encourage use of imagination (e.g. It could be: 'a giant fishing rod,' 'a scary dinosaur's leg bone,' 'a supersonic aeroplane').

- What kind of game could you play with the stick? (e.g. 'I could play Pooh Sticks.')

 Extension activity: Ask the pupils to make their own identification guide about the stick and the tree it came from. This should be no longer than three or four sentences and include a description and illustration of the tree or the leaf, or both (e.g. 'The birch tree is a deciduous tree. The bark of the tree is silver grey. It can grow to over 50 metres.').

 Recording/evidencing: Retain the pupils' sentences and amalgamate the sheets into a class book.

 Assessment methods: Assess the pupils' ability to create fiction and non-fiction sentences. Read the sentences with each pupil to allow for oral feedback. Record your observations from the class discussions.

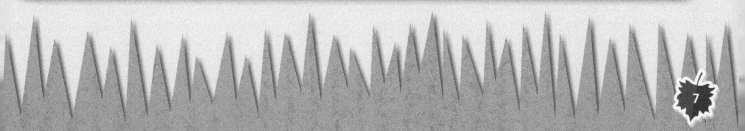

National Curriculum links

<u>Reading – comprehension</u>

- be encouraged to link what they read or hear read to their own experiences

- participate in discussion about what is read to them, taking turns and listening to what others say

<u>Writing – composition</u>

- sequence sentences to form short narratives

- discuss what they have written with the teacher or other pupils

Vocabulary	theme, empathy, imagine, sequence, sentence, thrive, native, habitat
Resources	a copy of *The Bog Baby* by Jeanne Willis; materials (small sticks, stones, pebbles, shells, leaves, flowers, blue feathers, wool); pictures drawn from *The Bog Baby*; flashcards, one of each (bog, dell, mud, bucket, tub, sick, fish, wings, jar, shed, shell, wool, wood, moon, pond, spring, frog, flower, sandpit, jump, sleep, chart); blue salt dough; paper and pencils; a camera or tablet device
Prior learning	class discussion
Cross-curricular links	Art – use a range of materials; Science – plants

Introduction

Read *The Bog Baby* by Jeanne Willis with the class. Talk about the themes in the story: How did Chrissy feel about the Bog Baby? What emotions did the Bog Baby display? Can the pupils think of a time when they felt the same way as Chrissy? Explain this is what we call 'empathy'.

Discuss what might have happened if the Bog Baby had not been returned – would there have been any more Bog Babies? What made the Bog Baby sick?

Talk about how we can look after nature, and how we should behave when we come across natural items that we love and want to keep.

Tell the pupils you would like them to imagine that the school grounds are now the Bluebell Woods, and that a Bog Baby has visited the school and has hidden words, pictures and materials from the story around the 'woods'. The pupils will need to look for the words and collect them as they go. Ask them to also look for places in the school grounds that the Bog Baby might like to live or play in.

Bog Baby stories

Before the activity begins, hide the pictures from the book, the flashcards and the materials around the school grounds.

As a class, go on a Bog Baby hunt. Explain to the pupils that there will be some pictures, word cards with words from the story, and materials that can be used to make their own Bog Babies. Ask pupils to collect all the cards, pictures and materials, and to bring them all back. Ask the pupils to read the words out loud.

Write the words: 'First', 'Next', 'Then' and 'Finally' on the playground or on paper, and place on the ground. As a class, ask the pupils to sequence the pictures and the word cards in the order that they appear in the story.

Provide blue salt dough and ask the pupils to create their own Bog Baby. Use the sticks, leaves and feathers to make a habitat in a natural setting for their Bog Babies. Photograph their work.

Give each pupil a sheet of paper, and ask them to think of a short story they could write about their Bog Baby. Help the pupils to write three short sentences using the prompts First, Next and Finally. Group the pupils together and ask them to share their short story.

 Extension activity: Look at an image of a bluebell woodland. Explain that the bluebell is a native wildflower, and has been voted the nation's favourite wildflower. But, like the Bog Baby, the bluebell needs a certain habitat to be able to grow and thrive. Ask the pupils if they have ever visited a bluebell wood, and seen the carpet of blue flowers, and smelt the perfume. Discuss bluebells and woodland trips as a class.

 Recording/evidencing: Collate the written sentences about the pupils' individual Bog Babies to display in a class Bog Baby book, along with photos of the Bog Babies and habitats.

 Assessment methods: Record any observations from the class discussions to assess if the pupils are linking what they have heard to their own experiences and their level of participation. Discuss each pupil's written work with them.

National Curriculum links

Writing – composition

- write for different purposes

- write sentences by:
  - saying out loud what they are going to write about
  - re-reading what they have written to check that it makes sense

Vocabulary	menu, sentence, ingredients, punctuation
Resources	restaurant menus that include three courses; waterproof aprons or coveralls; mud kitchen equipment per group (e.g. supply of mud in a small bucket or bowl; container of water; mixing bowls; old saucepans; old kitchen utensils; plastic jugs; selection of natural items to be used as 'ingredients', e.g. flowers, feathers, leaves, sticks, shells, pine cones, pebbles); a list of the 'ingredients' that have been supplied; metal or plastic plates and platters for serving; a large piece of card or paper (for the class menu); a large tarpaulin or picnic mat; a bowl of soapy water and some towels/wet wipes; paper, pencils and clipboard for each pupil; a camera or tablet device
Prior learning	thinking aloud, collecting ideas and drafting sentences
Cross-curricular links	Art – creating with varying materials; Maths – measurement; PSHE – working as a team

Introduction

Have a class discussion about cooking and preparing meals, snacks and treats. Ask the pupils what their favourite foods are and if they know what ingredients are in the meal. Look at restaurant menu examples, pointing out the different courses and how the menu includes a brief description or lists some of the ingredients.

Explain that they need to create an invitation for the head teacher to join them for a special treat. Ask the class to choose a name for their restaurant. Ask what they think the invitation should say.

Discuss how to create a sentence that is clear to the reader (e.g. 'Please come to the field and enjoy a special lunch at 1pm.'). Ask all the pupils to write a sentence, and then choose two pupils to deliver their examples.

Mud bake-off

Separate the pupils into three groups. Explain that they are going to create and use a mud kitchen and that one group will make starters, one will make main courses and the other will make desserts.

Give each group an area in which to work, and the mud kitchen equipment. Allow pupils to create and organise their mud kitchen. Explain that they need to make at least two options for the course they are responsible for (e.g. mud meatballs, muddy stew, mud spaghetti) and that they can use any ingredients they want. Emphasise that no muddy treats are to be eaten. Explain to the groups that they will need to write down the ingredients they use, copying the words from the list (e.g. mud, sticks, feathers).

Once they have made their dishes and written their ingredients list, each pupil in the group needs to say a sentence about one of the dishes and then write their sentence on their paper (e.g. 'Our dish is called Mud Pie and has mud, flowers and sticks in.'). They should make sure their sentences make sense, include the ingredients and use capital letters, commas and full stops. If they wish, they can include information about how much of an ingredient they have used (e.g. one bowl of mud, three flowers, two sticks).

A member from each group writes the name of their dishes on a class menu. The group chooses a sentence to go with each dish; this could be a group member's pre-prepared sentence or they could create a new sentence. Ask the group to re-read the sentences to check they make sense, include all the ingredients used and are correctly punctuated.

Choose an area of the grounds to place the tarpaulin/picnic mat – this will be the restaurant. Welcome the head teacher, give them the class menu and invite them to inspect the range of dishes and make their selections from the menu. All the pupils need to listen carefully to the selections and then the groups present their chosen dishes in turn, reading the name aloud and serving it to the head teacher.

At the end of the meal, explain that in restaurants the staff help to clean up – so begin Operation Clean-up!

 Extension activity: Ask the pupils to say a sentence aloud about the head teacher's visit, and then write that sentence.

 Recording/evidencing: Gather together written lists of ingredients, the sentences and the class menu. Take photos of the meals, the pupils' participation and the mess to display in class.

 Assessment methods: Listen to the pupils orally preparing their sentences about their dishes, and assess the written sentences with the pupils, to check they make sense and include the ingredients.

Story sequence

National Curriculum links

Spoken language

- give well-structured descriptions, explanations and narratives for different purposes, including for expressing feelings

- participate in discussions, presentations, performances, role play, improvisations and debates

Writing – composition

- sequence sentences to form short narratives

Vocabulary	sculpture, name, habitat, characteristics, features, adjectives, texture, consistency, descriptive sentence, class story
Resources	clay/wet mud or modelling/air drying clay; water; containers; stirring sticks; natural materials (e.g. leaves, small sticks, flowers, pine cones, stones and pebbles); a camera or tablet device; waterproof aprons or coveralls; tarpaulin; paper and pens; wet wipes
Prior learning	compose a sentence orally before writing it
Cross-curricular links	Art – use a range of materials; Science – animals including humans

Introduction

Ask pupils if they know of any stories featuring monsters, such as *The Gruffalo* and *Zog*, and discuss what features monsters can have. What are the pupils' favourite monsters? Which are the scariest monsters they can think of?

Clay monsters and story scribing

Gather the pupils in an area in the school grounds where there are some trees, sticks, leaves, stones and flowers (or bring a selection of these natural materials with you). Spread the tarpaulin on the ground and, with the pupils, make a mixture of clay/mud/ water in a big bowl. The final consistency should be like cake mixture. Encourage the pupils to describe what the mud feels like. Model words such as 'texture' and 'consistency', and talk together about what a descriptive sentence is (e.g. 'the mud is wet') and what a great descriptive sentence might look like (e.g. 'the mud is slippery, cool and squishy'). Allow the pupils to experiment and play with the mud, and provide sticks for any pupils who are not willing to touch it.

Spread out the selection of natural materials on the tarpaulin. Split the pupils into pairs or threes. Explain that they are going to make their own monster faces on the trees or other vertical surfaces. Reassure the pupils that there is no right or wrong version of a monster's face – it can have one eye or ten, it can be big or small. Explain the process for making the monsters:

- Take a large handful of the clay/mud mixture and slap it onto a vertical surface, then squish and sculpt it into whatever shape they want their monster's face to be.

- Select any of the natural materials and use them to add features to the faces, making sure the pupils are fair to each other about the quantities used.

Whilst they are making their faces, ask the pupils to think about a name and a habitat for their monster, as well as the characteristics it might have (e.g. what it likes to eat, whether it is friendly or scary). Allow the pupils 10–15 minutes to create their monster. Visit each group and discuss their creation and any thoughts they have about their monster's name, habitat and characteristics.

Ask the pupils, in their pairs or threes, to write a descriptive sentence about their monster.

As a group, sit down in a circle near to the monster collection and compose a class story about a monster. Explain that the story should have a beginning, a middle and an end, and that you will start the story, then the pupil to your left will continue by offering one sentence. Begin the story and go around the circle, asking the pupils to take turns to progress the story as you write down their sentences.

Give each pupil three small pieces of blank paper. Read out loud the class story and choose three short sentences at random. Ask pupils to write down each sentence on a different piece of paper, and then to place the sentences in the right order. Discuss with the pupils what the right order should be.

 Extension activity: Ask the pupils to write a short story of three or four sentences about their clay monster. Observe how well they sequence their stories.

 Recording/evidencing: Take photos of the clay monster faces to display in class or on the school website. Display the class story alongside photos of the clay faces. Include photos of the pupils engaged in the activity along with the sequenced sentences in their English book.

 Assessment methods: Listen to and observe the pupils as they make their monster faces and discuss ideas for their monster's name, habitat and characteristics. Look at the written sentences and assess the pupils' ability to write a descriptive sentence. Observe each pupil's ability to sequence the sentences correctly and their level of engagement in the discussions.

Exploring ideas

National Curriculum links

Spoken language

- use spoken language to develop understanding through speculating, hypothesising, imagining and exploring ideas

Reading – comprehension

- develop pleasure in reading, motivation to read, vocabulary and understanding

- make inferences on the basis of what is being said and done

Writing – composition

- write sentences by:
  - composing a sentence orally before writing it
  - re-reading what they have written to check that it makes sense

Vocabulary	Stone Age, dwelling, cave painting, extinct, illustrate, compare, sentence
Resources	a copy of *Cave Baby* by Julia Donaldson; waterproof jackets or overalls; turmeric, blackberries, small flakes of charcoal, spinach, mud to make paint (alternatively, classroom paint can be used and pupils can be encouraged to imagine the natural ingredients, e.g. 'imagine that this green paint is made of spinach leaves'); small beakers/plastic yoghurt pots; small sticks; variety of brushes; story stones (pre-painted, purchased or made by the pupils as part of the activity) with pictures of characters (mum, dad, baby) and animals (mammoth, tiger, bear, hare, hyena), punctuation marks (, . ! ?), words (romp, splash, spots, stars, stripy, wiggly, sleeping, woolly, curly, happy, restless), colours (brown, yellow, grey, brown), rhyming words (brave, cave, bear, there) and connective words (and, then, next); paper and pens; a camera or tablet device
Prior learning	listen and share ideas
Cross-curricular links	History – understanding past events; Art – using painting to develop and share ideas and develop imagination

Introduction

Explain that in the Stone Age, when Cave Baby was alive, humans lived in caves and used tools made from stone and bones, because they had no metal or plastic. Some of the animals that lived then are extinct now, while some still exist. The people had to go out and hunt or gather their own food – no shops! – and all paints and dyes came from the plants they found, like berries, or from earth or charcoal.

Read *Cave Baby* by Julia Donaldson together, and compare and contrast Cave Baby with a modern baby. How is Cave Baby different from a modern baby? Discuss clothing, home, environment and pets. How are they the same? Discuss boredom, feelings and rules. How do we feel, act or behave when we feel bored? How do Cave Baby's emotions mirror or differ from how we feel? How do we know what Cave Baby is feeling?

Explain that cave paintings were used for many things, including telling stories, passing on messages, warnings or advice and describing animals in the local area. People would move from place to place and, when they arrived somewhere new, this information was useful to them. Tell the class that they are going to pretend to be Cave Baby and create a wall painting. Discuss how paints were made differently, with natural ingredients.

Let's paint the cave!

Explain that you would like them to create a sentence about how Cave Baby feels. The sentence should start with 'Cave Baby likes …', 'Cave Baby is scared of …' or 'Cave Baby feels …'. Split the class into five groups. Listen to the pupils in their groups compose their sentences orally and, together with a teaching assistant, support each group to write their sentences down, then re-read and check that they make sense.

Explain that they are now going to paint a picture about their sentence. For example, if they have written that Cave Baby is scared of bears, they could paint the bear or a picture of Cave Baby looking scared. Check the pupils have their overalls on. Give each group a pot, a spoon, a small stick and a small amount of one of the following ingredients: blackberries, turmeric, charcoal (pre-crushed into small lumps), spinach or mud. Remind the class they should not eat the ingredients! Mix the ingredient with a small amount of water, using a stick to crush and mix the ingredients. Give each group some of each colour paint and ask them to paint their picture on a concrete wall or a wooden fence.

Once the paintings have been finished, gather the groups together and ask them what they think the other groups' pictures are showing and what their sentence might have said.

 Extension activity: Ask the pupils to select stones from the punctuation, picture and word stones. Challenge them to use the stones to retell the story from the point of view of baby, the bear or the mammoth.

 Recording/evidencing: Collect the written sentences and take photographs of the paintings. Listen to the oral composition of the group's sentences and individual participation in discussions, and record anything of significance.

 Assessment methods: Assess the pupils' ability to construct and write a sentence, and to check it makes sense.

Story pyramids

National Curriculum links

Reading – comprehension

- discuss the sequence of events in books and how items of information are related

Writing – composition

- consider what they are going to write before beginning by:
    - planning or saying out loud what they are going to write about
    - writing down ideas and/or key words, including new vocabulary
- make simple additions, revisions and corrections to their own writing by:
    - evaluating their writing with the teacher and other pupils
    - reading aloud what they have written with appropriate intonation to make the meaning clear

Vocabulary	characters, plot, resolution, story pyramid
Resources	a copy of *The Lorax* by Dr Seuss; A3 sheets; chalk; wooden lolly sticks; compost; wildflower seeds; permanent markers; story pyramid diagrams; pencils; a camera or tablet device
Prior learning	sequence of stories, creative writing
Cross-curricular links	Science – plants and seeds

Introduction

Read *The Lorax* by Dr Seuss as a class. Discuss the meaning, the characters, the plot and the resolution.

Explore the theory of a story pyramid:

- Line 1: the name of the character should be at the top of the pyramid
- Line 2: two words to describe the character
- Line 3: three words to describe the setting
- Line 4: four words stating the story problem
- Line 5: five words describing one event in the story
- Line 6: six words describing a second event
- Line 7: seven words describing a third event
- Line 8: eight words to describe the resolution.

Show the pupils a diagram to illustrate this, and take a printed copy of this and the book outside.

Building a pyramid

Discuss the elements of the story pyramid and how *The Lorax* fits this model. Challenge the pupils to work in groups to create their own story pyramids for *The Lorax* on A3 sheets. Allow 15 minutes for this activity. Make sure the pupils have access to the story pyramid structure, either by being near the diagram or by having a printed copy.

Ask each group to share their ideas and explain their story pyramid to the other groups. Encourage each group to listen to the comments and suggestions made, and to revise and correct their pyramid as needed.

Using either pencils and A3 paper or chalk on the playground, ask pupils to work in groups to create their own story using the story pyramid and outside environment as inspiration. Come together as a class and share some of these stories.

 Extension activity: As a class, create a story using the story pyramid principle. Ensure the story is planned according to the story pyramid rule, and use the theme of 'Caring for our school environment'. Once the story is complete, arrange an outdoor performance for an assembly. Split the class into small groups and divide the lines of the pyramid among them to perform.

 Recording/evidencing: Observe the pupils working, and retain their group pyramids and stories for a display in school. Video the class story or ask the pupils to present and discuss their activity in an assembly, share with the rest of the school and add to the school website.

 Assessment methods: Assess the group story pyramids and stories with the groups of pupils, asking them to self-evaluate how their story fits with the structure. Assess with the pupils if the pyramid concept has helped them to understand how to structure a story.

Fairy tales

National Curriculum links

Reading – comprehension:

- become very familiar with key stories, fairy stories and traditional tales, retell them and consider their particular characteristics

- recognise and join in with predictable phrases

Spoken language

- maintain attention and participate actively in collaborative conversations, staying on topic and initiating and responding to comments

- use spoken language to develop understanding through speculating, hypothesising, imagining and exploring ideas

- speak audibly and fluently

Vocabulary	fairy tale, repeated phrases, predict, sequence, performance, setting, characters
Resources	a copy of *The Three Little Pigs*; rope; cards with 'Once upon a time' (one card), 'then' (five cards), and 'and' (five cards); at least six pictures from the story of *The Three Little Pigs*; straw, sticks, small clamps or pegs to hold the sticks together if needed, play bricks or boxes; leaves; a camera or tablet device
Prior learning	familiarity with traditional fairy tales
Cross-curricular links	Science – animals; Design and technology – design and make

Introduction

Discuss with the class what they think a fairy tale is and whether they can name one. Tell the pupils the story of *The Three Little Pigs*, pausing and prompting the pupils to join in with the repeated phrases and to predict what will happen next.

Tell me a tale

Take the pupils outside. Show them the 'Once upon a time', 'then' and 'and' cards. Lay the rope out in a straight line and ask the pupils to arrange the pictures from *The Three Little Pigs* along the rope, sequencing the word cards so the story makes sense.

Split the pupils into three groups. Explain that each group will represent one of the three little pigs. Assign each group an area within the school grounds and give them either straw, sticks or some play bricks or boxes, depending on which pig they are, to make a small house or a larger den-type structure. Allow them to use their imaginations and be creative! They can use the pegs to help hold the sticks together if needed, and the straw could be piled into a house shape.

Each group, with a teaching assistant or with you, should discuss their pig: how they might have made their house, why they might have chosen that material and what it would have looked like. The pupils could embellish the character and name the pig, if desired. Encourage all pupils to participate actively and to speak clearly.

Gather all the class together and explain that you are going to be the wolf. Visit each house, and ask the pupils to share with you what they discussed about their pig.

After the discussion, give all the pupils some leaves to throw into the wind as they all say the phrase 'then he huffed and he puffed and he blew (or couldn't blow) the house down!' Then visit the next house.

When all the houses have been visited, read the story again, encouraging the pupils to join in with the 'huffed and puffed' sections.

 Extension activity: Challenge the class to come up with their own versions of the fairy tale. Encourage them to experiment with elements of the tale such as characters, sequence or setting. Allow them to use the picture cards and rope to mix up the settings or sequence of their story.

 Recording/evidencing: Take photographs of the pupils sequencing the story, and/or video the pupils in their groups discussing their pig and the final re-enactment; these can be shared on the class page of the school website.

 Assessment methods: Observe the group sharing the information about their character and how individuals participate in the group discussions and the retelling of *The Three Little Pigs*. Include photographs of individuals and your comments from the activity in their English books.

Phonic forest

National Curriculum links

Reading – word reading

- apply phonic knowledge and skills as the route to decode words

Vocabulary	phonics, grapheme, phoneme
Resources	clipboards, paper, pencils; 'phonics forest trees' – find five trees to hang pre-prepared cards on (pupils need to be able to reach the cards; if this is not possible, lay the cards around the tree)
	example real words for cards (two per pupil): long, soil, crab, chart, scrap, river, scram, beehive, chin, queen, forest, haunt, main, brown, crowds, fund, think, doom, splat, fuel
	example alien words (two per pupil): shog, thard, harnd, frem, jat, vol, yewn, clain, jair, zale, blurns, skarld, jorb, zulp, oth, shan, drap, flarm, voisk, braft
	two more trees – one with a large 'Real' sign on it, and the other decorated with cards showing aliens (or a fake tree with a 'Not Real' sign)
Prior learning	phonics work
Cross-curricular links	PE – team games

Introduction

Revisit and revise some recent phonics work with the class – play a game where you call out some high frequency words (the, and, her, had, etc.) and the pupils write the words down.

Explain that the school grounds have been visited by a naughty nonsense alien who has set the pupils a challenge of finding the real words and the alien words.

The word in the woods

Make sure each pupil has a clipboard, paper and a pencil. Split the pupils into five groups, and start each group at a different tree. Remind the pupils to sound out the words using their phonic knowledge, to blend the sound and to think about whether it is a correct/real word, or if it is incorrect/alien. Challenge the pupils to independently write down on their sheets the real words from the trees.

When they think they have written down all the real words and are ready to move on to the next tree, they raise their hands. When all groups have finished, ask them to move on to the next tree.

Once the pupils have completed all five trees, bring them together in the playground and discuss and share answers.

Ask each pupil to go back to a word tree and collect two alien words and two real ones. They hang their words on the real tree or the alien tree. As a class, check that all the words are on the correct tree.

 Extension activity: Draw five different hopscotch grids with the words being spelt at the top:

- a grid with six boxes and the letters from the word 'forest' in the grid

- a grid with seven boxes and the letters from the word 'beehive'

- a grid with five boxes and the letters from the word 'scram'

- a grid with five boxes and the letters from the word 'brown'

- a grid with eight boxes and the letters from the word 'midnight'.

Ask pupils to take turns to firstly spell out the words by jumping on the letters in the correct order, and then to make up their own alien word by jumping on the letters out of order. If there is time, allow pupils to have a turn on each grid.

 Recording/evidencing: Collect the written collections of real words, and take photos of the real and alien trees.

 Assessment methods: Assess pupils' answers and collections and recognition of the real words, and assess their ability to use phonic knowledge to decode the words.

Noun phrases

National Curriculum links

<u>Writing – vocabulary, grammar and punctuation</u>

- learn how to use expanded noun phrases to describe and specify [for example, the blue butterfly]

Vocabulary	noun, noun phrases, descriptive word
Resources	A3 paper with the headings 'People', 'Places', 'Things'; blank pieces of A4 paper or card in four colours; plastic wallets and string; washing line and pegs; paper, pencils and clipboards for each pupil; a camera or tablet device
Prior learning	creative writing, recognition of nouns, noun phrase
Cross-curricular links	Science – people and animals

Introduction

Revisit the definition of noun. Play a 'Longest List' game with pupils. Divide the class into four groups, and give each group a sheet of A3 paper with the headings 'People', 'Places' and 'Things' and a pencil. Give each group two minutes to think of and write down nouns under each category and see which group has the longest list.

Nouns in the grounds!

Split the class into two groups and give each pupil a clipboard, a piece of paper and a pencil. Ask each group to walk around the school grounds with a supervising adult and to write a list of all the nouns that they can find. Encourage pupils to include examples of people, places and things. Allow 10 minutes for the exploratory walk.

Ask the pupils to work together in their groups to split the nouns into the three categories (people, places, things). Provide each group with sheets of coloured card or paper and have one pupil in each group write two or three examples of people on one colour, places on another colour and things on a third colour. Place the cards into the plastic wallets and place them in a pile on the ground.

Find two vertical objects to tie a washing line to (between two trees is ideal). With the class sitting together as one group, ask a volunteer to take one card and think of a descriptive word to add to it. Explain that this makes a noun phrase. Ask the pupil to write their descriptive word on a blank card and to hang the cards on the washing line. Take a photo of the pupil's noun phrase and then put the noun back in the pile and invite another volunteer to repeat the activity. Allow all pupils to have a go.

Extension activity: Choose three or four of the pupils' noun phrases and use them to collaboratively create a class poem or story using the following structure.

Outside, we can see a ....

Can you find the ....?

Look! There is a ....

Then finish with a question or comment.

 Recording/evidencing: The photos of the pupils' noun phrases can be printed and included in their books and displayed in the classroom.

 Assessment methods: Assess each pupil's understanding of noun phrases.

Creating a travel guide

National Curriculum links

<u>Spoken language</u>

- give well-structured descriptions, explanations and narratives for different purposes, including for expressing feelings

<u>Writing – composition</u>

- develop positive attitudes towards and stamina for writing by:
  - writing for different purposes
- consider what they are going to write before beginning by:
  - writing down ideas and/or key words, including new vocabulary

Vocabulary	description, feature, identification, non-fiction, genre
Resources	clipboards; paper made into small pre-prepared books with 10–16 pages (one book per group of four pupils); pencils; squared paper; cameras or tablet devices; blank postcards; post-it notes; tree and plant identification guides; small pieces of paper, sticks, pebbles, string; local area guides or pre-printed satellite images of school area from a website; maps
Prior learning	exposure to differing genres of texts
Cross-curricular links	Geography – use aerial photographs and plan perspectives to recognise landmarks and basic human and physical features, devise a simple map, and use and construct basic symbols in a key; Science – plants

Introduction

Show the pupils a travel guide for their local area. Look at what it includes and discuss if the pupils have been to any of the places the guide describes. Look at an example of travel guides for children (e.g. *ZigZag City Guides*) and look at how the guide includes a map and a list of interesting features and places to visit. Discuss how the places included are made to sound exciting.

Explain that you are going to create an informative travel guide and a map of the school for any visitors. Brainstorm the best way to display the information. Would pupils like to add descriptions or interesting points about the areas in the school? How would this information be offered? Should they use postcards similar to the ZigZag cards? Or stick their notes into the pre-prepared books?

Type the school postcode into the website http://gridreferencefinder.com/ and find the location of the school. (If you see a diagrammatic map, click on the Satellite button in the top left corner of the image.) Explain that the image is taken by a satellite in space. Print a copy for each group.

Guide to school!

Divide the class into four groups and assign each group an area in the school grounds. Provide each group with paper, clipboard, post-it notes, blank postcards, a pre-prepared book, pencils and a camera or tablet device. Ask the pupils to explore their section of the grounds and to:

- draw points of interest, and mark out green spaces, plants and trees
- identify any special features of the area (e.g. playground equipment, a good place to make dens, their wildlife area, the sports field)
- use tree and plant identification guides to name any trees or plants they can
- add labels to identify the areas (e.g. playground, field, lining-up areas)
- take photographs of things the pupils think other people would be interested in visiting.

Ask them to draw and write on post-it notes and stick these onto their map in the correct places.

Ask each group to use the information on the post-it notes to write a description of an area. This could be done on postcards, in a style like that of the *ZigZag City Guides*.

Explain to the pupils that they are now tour guides and they must guide another group around their mapped section, pointing out and naming areas of interest, their features and naming any plants and trees as the journey progresses.

Collate the written work, photographs and maps to create a School Guide.

 Extension activity: Find a grassy area and explain that you would like the pupils, in their four groups, to make a simple 3-D map of their school. Allow the pupils to use small sticks, pebbles, string and their own creativity to recreate the school grounds. Allow around 15 minutes for the activity.

 Recording/evidencing: Photograph the groups as they explore and record the school grounds. Publish the photos and the School Guide on the school website, and display a copy in the school reception.

 Assessment methods: Assess each pupil's contribution to the travel guides, looking specifically for new vocabulary, key words and an understanding of the genre.

National Curriculum links

Writing – composition

- develop positive attitudes towards and stamina for writing by:
  - writing narratives about personal experiences and those of others (real and fictional)

Writing – vocabulary, grammar and punctuation

- learn how to use sentences with different forms: statement

Vocabulary	genre, fiction, non-fiction, story, fact, character, description, factual, statement, identification, characteristics
Resources	two different types of tree identification guides or printed tree information sheets (e.g. from the Woodland Trust or Forestry Commission); the Forestry Commission's *Tree Stories* publication (available as a free pdf download from the Forestry Commission website); blankets to sit on for creative writing exercise; paper, pencils and pens (Note: If none of the tree species are found in the school grounds, a sapling can be easily and cheaply purchased, and planted by the class as part of the lesson.)
Prior learning	writing for different purposes
Cross-curricular links	Science – plants; Geography – map work

Introduction

Show the class the copy of *Tree Stories* and look at the tree species featured.

Explain to the pupils that they are going to make their own tree facts and tree stories based on a tree found in the school grounds. To do this, they will need to know more about that tree and have a closer look at it.

Tree tales

Take the pupils around the school grounds and see if they can identify one of the species from *Tree Stories*. Ask the pupils to discuss its characteristics: height, size, leaf shape and colours, and fruit.

Divide the class into four groups. Each group should choose a different tree featured in the story book; Groups 1 and 2 each read to the class facts about their tree as given in the identification guides. Groups 3 and 4 each read aloud a story about their tree from *Tree Stories*. Discuss how both books are discussing the trees, but that one style is fiction and the other is factual or non-fiction.

Distribute paper, pens and pencils and ask two groups to write their own tree short story and the other two groups to write facts about their tree. The stories should include a character and a description of the tree, describe a short incident and be no longer than a page. The factual writing should include statements and facts about the tree and its surroundings, and also be no longer than a page.

 Extension activity: Look at the illustrations, pictures and diagrams in the books. On a separate page, ask the pupils to create an observational drawing of their tree, including its leaf, branch and fruit (depending on the season) to include with their story or factual account.

 Recording/evidencing: Publish the written work and illustrations on the school website to share with parents.

 Assessment methods: Read the stories and statements about the trees with the pupils to assess their understanding of the differences between the two genres.

Styles of poetry

National Curriculum links

Writing – composition

- develop positive attitudes towards and stamina for writing by:
  - o writing poetry

Vocabulary	poetry, kenning, descriptive, metaphor
Resources	paper and pens; chalk; five 'sense' trays containing a variety of items (see activity); two or three magnifying glasses
Prior learning	nouns
Cross-curricular links	Art – use drawing, painting and sculpture to develop and share their ideas, experiences and imagination

Introduction

Explain that a kenning is a device that is sometimes used for effect in poetry. It is the process of using a two-word phrase in place of a one-word noun. The Anglo-Saxon poem 'Beowulf' uses many kennings, for example:

- bone-house – body

- battle-light – sword

- wave-floater – ship

- whale-road – sea

- gold-friend – king

Read an extract from a child-friendly version of 'Beowulf' to the class and help pupils to find other examples of kennings.

Explain that a kennings poem is a riddle that is made up of several lines of kennings. Think of some examples together of kennings poems about the school or a local garden or wood. For example, a kenning about a flower could be:

- sunshine-swallower

- honey-helper

- colour-explosion.

Feel write

Separate the class into five groups. Set up stations around the school grounds to represent the five senses, for example:

- The 'touch' station could have a tray with wet mud, some bark, soft grass and pine cones, and perhaps some concrete as a contrast.

- The 'smell' station could have some scented herbs like rosemary or lavender, some rotting leaves or organic matter, and some cut grass.

- The 'taste' area could have some cooled herbal tea, soft edible berries and crunchy apples.

- The 'sight' area could include magnifying glasses on a patch of grass, with some leaves and flowers, or be in a pleasant area of the school grounds.

- The 'hearing' area could include large sea shells, leaves to break up and small sticks to snap.

Ask each group to visit each station. The groups should select a single item from one of the stations and write a three-line kenning poem about it – without naming the item!

Once the groups have written their poems, ask them to share their work with the class; the other groups try to guess the item the poem describes.

Scribe all the poems on to a flip chart or ask the pupils to write their poems.

 Extension activity: Divide the class into four groups. Ask two groups to create a kenning poem about their classroom and the other two groups to create a kenning poem about a lesson outside. Ask the pupils to write their poems down.

 Recording/evidencing: Encourage the pupils to decorate the poem they wrote at the senses station, or the group poem. Keep the class poem and group poems as evidence.

 Assessment methods: Observe the level of participation, contributions and understanding of kennings by each pupil throughout the activity.

Report writing

National Curriculum links

Spoken language

- use relevant strategies to build their vocabulary

Reading – comprehension

- discuss and clarify the meanings of words, linking new meanings to known vocabulary

Writing – composition

- develop positive attitudes towards and stamina for writing by:
  - o writing about real events
- consider what they are going to write before beginning by:
  - o planning or saying out loud what they are going to write about
  - o writing down ideas and/or key words, including new vocabulary

Vocabulary	habitat, needs, report, features, headings, language, investigation
Resources	empty picture frame sized A4 or larger; plant and insect identification guide; clipboards and paper (A3 works well outdoors for handwriting when sitting in a cross-legged position); pre-prepared habitat sheets (see activity); pencils; an example of a report
Prior learning	Science – habitats
Cross-curricular links	Science – animals, including humans and scientific enquiry

Introduction

Explain what a habitat is. What do humans need in a habitat? Explain that the school is one kind of physical environment surrounding the school population. What do we humans need to *survive*, and what do we need to *thrive*? Make a list with pupils, discussing shelter, warmth, food, sunshine, exercise and companionship.

What do insects, animals and plants need in a habitat? Discuss basic needs for survival, such as sunshine and rain. What animals might visit the school grounds? What insects and plants might live there? What do they need to survive, and what do they need to thrive? What impact do we have on their habitat in our school and how can we reduce it (e.g. by creating habitats for insects, by making sure small animals have enough water, by not picking leaves or damaging plants and by not littering)?

Read aloud or show the pupils an example of a report. Discuss how a report differs from a story – for example, look at the headings; think about how the language is different from the language found in a story; consider why and when would we need a report.

Tell the class that they are going to be explorers and conduct an investigation. Ask: 'What is an explorer? What is an investigation and how can we record what we find? What will we need as explorers?' Discuss methods of investigating and recording with pupils. The pupils will use the results of their explorations to write a report about their school grounds as a habitat for nature.

Our school habitat

Ask the pupils to explore the school grounds and count how many different habitats they can find. Ask them to list the features, and predict and observe what living things are there. Take the pupils to as many different areas as possible (e.g. a grassy area, a planted area, a concrete or playground environment and a wildlife or pond area). Provide pre-prepared sheets with the headings: 'Introduction' (this should include sentence starters for a description of the habitat), 'What grows here?' and 'What lives here?'. Ask the pupils to write key words under each heading.

Explain to the pupils that they will use the empty area inside the picture frame to investigate and count the different insects and plants they can find. Are there any signs of animals? Record the names of the plants and insects they find in each area and how many plants and insects there are. Discuss why the creatures live there and what benefits those habitats have for the animals.

Ask the pupils to use their notes to write a report on the habitats, using the headings to structure it.

Extension activity: Allow the pupils some time to review and then write a copy of their report in their best writing, and to add one sentence – 'To make our school grounds even better I would …'.

Recording/evidencing: The pupil's individual reports are evidence.

Assessment methods: Assess each pupil's understanding of writing a report by reading with the individual pupils. Record any significant observations of discussions, vocabulary enrichment and involvement of pupils during the activity.

National Curriculum links

Number – number and place value

- identify and represent numbers using objects and pictorial representations including the number line, and use the language of: equal to, more than, less than (fewer), most, least

Measurement

- compare, describe and solve practical problems for lengths and heights

- measure and begin to record lengths and heights

Vocabulary	equal to, more than, less than, equals, measure, tall, taller, tallest, taller than
Resources	three metre sticks or measuring tapes; chalk; three long cardboard tubes (approx. 1 metre – old wrapping paper cardboard tubes are ideal) and three blocks to rest the tubes on to create a ramp; selection of small toy cars (three per group); one number line per pupil; a camera or tablet device
Prior learning	measuring in centimetres
Cross-curricular links	Technology – structures, design and make

Introduction

Divide the class into three groups. Give each group a metre stick or measuring tape, and ask them to measure the height of one of the group's members. Record the results on the board. Ask the class which pupil's height measurement is the largest number, and which is the smallest number. Then ask each group to compare the heights, using the language of equal to, less than and more than.

Ready, steady, race!

Ask each group to prop their cardboard tube up on their block to create a ramp, and to put their metre stick/measuring tape on the floor at the end of the tube and to mark zero on the playground where it starts. Explain that the pupils are going to race some toy cars and then measure how far the cars travel.

Ask each group to launch their three cars in turn down the tube, chalking a mark where each car travels to on the playground (recording the front of the car). The winning vehicle is the one that travels the furthest; give that distance a chalk star mark. Talk about how letting the cars go instead of pushing them will ensure the test is fair. After the races are completed, there should be three winning cars, one from each group. Help the pupils to measure the distances to the star marks that the winning cars travelled to.

Gather the pupils together. Give each pupil a 1–100 number line, and ask them to mark each winning car's distance on the line. If the measurement is greater than 100cm, ask the pupils to write the number at the end of the number line. Discuss the distance each winning car travelled: whether each distance is greater than, less than or equal to the distances achieved by the other two winning cars. Write the results on a chart, or use chalk to record them on the playground.

 Extension activity: Hold the races again, and record where each vehicle stops. Sort the cars into first, second and third places.

Finish with a game: measure and mark with chalk a metre-long line for each group. Call out measurements (e.g. 25cm, 50cm, 90cm) and ask the pupils to estimate where the measurement will be on the line, and then to measure and see how accurate they were.

 Recording/evidencing: Pupils will have their number lines as a record. Photograph the results chart. Record pupils' participation, and take photos to annotate.

 Assessment methods: Observe the activity, and assess the pupils' confidence in measuring accurately. Assess the pupils' understanding of equal to, less than and more than.

Creating tally charts

National Curriculum links

Number – number and place value
- count in steps of 2, 3 and 5 from 0
- compare and order numbers from 0 up to 100; use <, > and = signs

Statistics
- interpret and construct simple tally charts

Vocabulary	table, tally, fieldwork, record, data, compare, measure
Resources	images of worms; four measuring tapes or metre sticks; chalk; watering can; kitchen forks; sticks of around 10mm diameter and around 10cm length; small garden forks; paper and pencils; stopwatch; four tubs or containers
Prior learning	counting in fives, recording data
Cross-curricular links	Science – animals; Geography – study of a small area and fieldwork

Introduction

In the classroom make a tally chart of the number of pupils in the class, reinforcing counting in fives.

Look at pictures of earthworms and discuss their usual habitat. Discuss facts about earthworms (e.g. earthworms like to eat soil, roots and leaves; they have no teeth and a tiny mouth; they like dark, moist conditions; they help the soil by adding nutrients through their poo).

Discuss how worms should be handled, and explain that pupils are going to participate in some 'worm charming'. Explain that the worms will come out from the soil when the ground is vibrated (or shaken). Ask the pupils about ways they could do this. Split the pupils into four groups and ask them to think of a suitable name for their group.

Worm charming

Take the pupils outside and give each group a metre stick or measuring tape. Help the pupils to mark out four 3m × 3m plots on a soil surface (ideally, in a piece of ground that you've already checked has worms). Use the chalk to create a large four-column table on the playground or on a fence, and write the name of each group at the top of each column.

The pupils are now going to charm the worms from the ground. Allocate one of the following methods to each group:

- watering the ground, and stamping and jumping
- putting a selection of kitchen forks into the ground and tapping lightly on them with a small stone
- putting one stick into the ground and using another stick to hit the top
- using the garden forks to make holes in the ground.

Explain that no digging is allowed and that pupils must stop moving when asked. Give each group a piece of paper and a pencil, and explain that they will make a tally chart to record how many worms they collect.

Allow the pupils 2–3 minutes to make as much vibration as they can, and then pause for one minute. Each worm should be gently picked up by hand and collected into the containers and given 1 mark on the tally chart. Continue for 10–15 minutes. Record the results and ask the pupils to set their worms free.

Gather the class together and ask one pupil from each group to record their results in their column on the table, counting and recording the tally in groups of five. As a class, add up the totals by counting in fives.

 Extension activity: Compare the results. Who charmed the most worms, and why do pupils think that was? Ask the pupils to record which team was first, second, third and fourth, and the results for each team. Talk about which is the greatest and the smallest number, and which team had more than or less than the other teams. Compare the results using the =, < and > signs, and write appropriate statements on the board.

 Recording/evidencing: Photocopy the teams' results sheets, and stick into each pupil's maths book.

 Assessment methods: Use the tally charts to check that pupils have understood how to count in fives.

Exploring 2-D shapes

National Curriculum links

<u>Geometry – properties of shapes</u>

* recognise and name common 2-D shapes

Vocabulary	2-D shapes polygon, vertex, vertices, side, rectangle, triangle, circle
Resources	pictures of 2-D shapes; images of everyday items; lengths of wool or string approximately 20cm long (1 per pupil); four lengths of rope approximately 10m each; variety of stones of differing sizes, with straight lines or vertices drawn on them with a white marker or paint (suggested, 30 stones with lines, 25 with vertices); a camera or tablet device
Prior learning	recognition of polygons
Cross-curricular links	Art – creating shape pictures and using different materials

Introduction

Show the pupils pictures of 2-D shapes and discuss the name of the shape and the number of sides each shape has. Then show them images of everyday items (e.g. a house, a road sign, a clock), and look for shapes within them. Ask pupils to draw an example of each shape. Discuss which shapes have four sides and straight sides, and where the vertices are.

Sorting stones

Choose four pupils and ask them to stand so that each of them is at the vertex of a square with sides approximately 10m long; use the lengths of rope to connect the pupils. Ask the pupils to place the rope square on the ground, securing it with small stones. Play a game, calling out for the pupils to stand: in a vertex, by a side, inside or outside the square. Explain that any shape with straight sides is called a polygon. Repeat the game for a rectangle, a triangle and a circle, changing the commands in the game appropriately.

Split the pupils into small groups and give each pupil a length of wool or string. Demonstrate how to create string shapes and then ask pupils to make their own.

Give each group a selection of stones with lines and vertices drawn on, and encourage the pupils to experiment with making shapes with the stones (e.g. select four stones with straight lines and four vertices to make a rectangle or square). Ask each group to use their stones to create a collection of triangles and non-triangles, four-sided shapes and not four-sided shapes. Allow five minutes for this activity then, as a class, look at each of the shapes and name them. Talk about why it was not possible to make a circle.

 Extension activity: As a group, collect the stones. The pupils should place the stones together so the lines meet, and use them to make one large shape on the playground.

 Recording/evidencing: Take photos of the pupils making the shapes with the stones. Include these photos in their maths books and label the photos with your observations and any comments from the pupil.

 Assessment methods: When pupils are working, observe their knowledge and understanding of 2-D shapes.

Exploring quarters

National Curriculum links

Number – fractions

- recognise, find and name a half as one of two equal parts of an object, shape or quantity

- recognise, find and name a quarter as one of four equal parts of an object, shape or quantity

Notes and guidance (non-statutory)

- connect halves and quarters to the equal sharing and grouping of sets of objects and to measures, as well as recognising and combining halves and quarters as parts of a whole

Vocabulary	half, halving, quarter, equal parts, whole
Resources	chalk; sticks or garden canes; selection of leaves, pebbles, bean seeds or pine cones (enough for 10 objects per pair of pupils); rulers; paper, pencils; a camera or tablet device
Prior learning	recognise, find and name a half as one of two equal parts of an object, shape or quantity
Cross-curricular links	PE – movement patterns

Introduction

Line the pupils up, ready to go outside. Divide the line into two groups and explain that each group is one half of the line, then divide into four groups and explain that each group is one quarter of the line. If there is an odd number of pupils and/or the total number is not divisible by four, ask the remaining pupils to help divide the line into the groups.

Fractions in action

Divide the class into pairs and give each pair some chalk. Arrange the pebbles, leaves, bean seeds and pine cones on the playground, and ask each pair to collect a set of 10 objects. On the playground, ask each pair to use the chalk to draw a dividing line no longer than the size of a ruler (provide a ruler if needed), and to equally share the objects between the two sections. Ask how many are in each section. Repeat this with 8, 6, 4 and 2 objects, and explain that they are halving the collection.

Collect and lay out on the playground a selection of sticks, ideally straight and of differing sizes. If sticks are not readily available, bring in garden canes or sticks for the activity. Challenge the pupils to use the sticks to create a fraction collection/wall: ask them to place one long stick at the top of their collection, then two smaller sticks which together are roughly the same length as the first stick beneath it. Explain that each of the smaller sticks represents half of the longer stick, then ask them to place four smaller sticks underneath, which represent four quarters.

Provide chalk or pencil and paper, and ask the pupils to label each of the lines with the fraction to check understanding.

 Extension activity: Working in pairs and using the pebbles, leaves, bean seeds and pine cones, challenge the pupils with the following questions:

1. If a half of the collection of objects is 6, how many objects are in the whole collection?

2. If a half of a collection is 2, how many objects are in the whole collection?

3. If a whole collection has 20 objects, how many objects are in a quarter?

4. If a whole collection has 10 objects, how many objects make up half the collection?

The pupils must use their objects to make the answer, e.g. if the answer is 4, they must set out 4 objects. Once all the questions have been answered, photograph the results.

 Recording/evidencing: Photograph or film the pupils creating their collections of objects and stick arrangements. Photograph the answers in the extension activity.

 Assessment methods: Take photos of the pupils' fraction collections and observe their understanding of recognising and naming halves and quarters. Look at the photographs of the answers in the extension activity to assess understanding of half, quarter and whole. Print the photos and annotate them with the pupils and stick in their maths books.

National Curriculum links

Geometry – position and direction
- order and arrange combinations of mathematical objects in patterns and sequences

Number – number and place value (non-statutory)
- using materials and a range of representations, pupils practise counting, reading, writing and comparing numbers to at least 100 and solving a variety of related problems to develop fluency … pupils are introduced to larger numbers to develop further their recognition of patterns within the number system and represent them in different ways, including spatial representations

Vocabulary	sequence, pattern, rule
Resources	images of the Fibonacci sequence in nature (e.g. number of petals [5, 8, 13] on certain flowers, the scales on a pine cone, sea shells, a beehive); natural materials found in school grounds (e.g. flowers, feathers, leaves, sticks and pebbles); examples of Andy Goldsworthy's art; chalk; a camera or tablet device
Prior learning	commutative addition, place value on number lines
Cross-curricular links	Art – work of other artists

Introduction

Explain that a sequence is also a pattern. Model a pattern of images or items (e.g. pencil, chalk, book, pencil, chalk, book) and a number pattern (e.g. 0, 2, 4, 6, 8). Explain to the pupils that the first of these patterns is a repeating pattern and the second is a growing pattern.

Introduce the Fibonacci sequence, explaining that it is a really interesting number pattern. Show the class what the start of the pattern looks like (0, 1, 1, 2, 3, 5, …) and ask pupils if they can work out what the next number might be. (8) Explain that the rule is add the two numbers next to each other to get the next one. Ask pupils what the next number would be (13). Explain that the Fibonacci sequence can be seen in nature, and show images of this.

Pattern-worthy numbers

Split the pupils into four or five groups. Ask them to find a selection of natural materials and to use them to create a straight-line growing pattern on the playground (e.g. two leaves, three feathers). Ask the pupils to use chalk to write the number of items under the pattern.

Give each group a set of growing number patterns (e.g. 1, 2, 3, 4 and 2, 4, 6, 8) and ask the pupils to recreate the patterns using natural materials.

Show the pupils some relevant examples of Andy Goldsworthy's art. Ask them to create their own examples of natural art in their groups, using the items they have collected. Encourage them to focus on patterns that are found in the natural world such as flower petals, shells and spiders' webs (show pictures or draw an example on a wall or fence with chalk if necessary).

 Extension activity: Play a variation of the 'Duck, Duck, Goose' game. Split the pupils into three or four groups and select one pupil per group to be the 'caller'. Ask each group to sit in a circle. Ask the caller to walk around the circle, tapping each pupil on the head as they pass, and calling out a set pattern – for example, duck, duck; goose, goose; duck, duck; swan. The person who has been tapped and named swan needs to run around the circle in the opposite direction and try to get to the empty space before the caller does. Then agree a number pattern with the pupils, deciding together which number to use as the trigger to run (e.g. 1; 1, 2; 1, 2, 3; 1, 2, 3, 4; 1, 2, 3, 4, 5 [5 would be the trigger]). Allow each pupil to have a turn as the 'caller'.

 Recording/evidencing: Take photographs of the created patterns. Stick these photographs in the individual pupil's maths books.

 Assessment methods: Observe the pupils' understanding of sequences, and their ability to recreate and continue patterns.

Position, movement and rotation

National Curriculum links

Geometry – position and direction

- Year 1: describe position, direction and movement, including whole, half, quarter and three-quarter turns

- Year 2: describe position, direction and movement, including movement in a straight line, and distinguishing between rotation as a turn and in terms of right angles for quarter, half and three-quarter turns (clockwise and anticlockwise)

Vocabulary	maze, rotation, direction, forward, backward, rotate, right, left, half turn, quarter turn, three-quarter turn, whole turn, clockwise, anti-clockwise
Resources	images of mazes; equipment to create a maze (e.g. lengths of rope, chalk, boxes); scarfs for blindfolds; a poster with direction words; paper, pencils; a camera or tablet device
Prior learning	distance, direction – describe position, direction and movement, including whole, half, quarter and three-quarter turns
Cross-curricular links	Art – using a range of materials

Introduction

Discuss what a maze is (use images to assist) and ask if pupils have had any experience of being in a maze. How did they find the centre and how did they get out? What are the characteristics of a maze? Discuss how a maze could be made in the playground or school field.

Amazing mazes

Line the pupils up across the playground. Give them instructions to move across the playground, using language of direction such as forward, right and left.

Then model a rotation, in both directions. Describe and show the pupils a half turn, a quarter turn, a three-quarter turn and a whole turn clockwise and anti-clockwise, then call out those turns and ask the pupils to turn appropriately.

Split the pupils into groups of three or four. Ask each group to create a simple maze in a flat area of the school field or playground (top tip – a simple circle maze works well). They will need to create a path that leads to the centre and has four or more sharp bends and at least one dead end. Give them equipment to use to mark paths wide enough to walk through.

Show the pupils a poster with the direction words. One member of the group should be blindfolded and another member should hold the blindfolded person's elbow for safety; they will act only as eyes and not lead them. The rest of the group call out to guide the blindfolded person through the maze to the end of the path, using language such as forward, backward, rotate to the left/right, quarter, half, three-quarter and whole turns clockwise and anti-clockwise. Allow time for all pupils to do this.

Ask the pupils to write on paper the directions to the centre of their maze. For example, 'Take three steps forward, then a quarter turn clockwise (or to the right). Then take two steps forward and make a half turn anticlockwise (or to the left).'

 Extension activity: The pupils give their written directions to another group and see if the other group can use the instructions to reach the centre. Play a game where the pupils follow the directions you call. For example, 'Take 10 steps forward. Run to the left side of the playground.'

 Recording/evidencing: Document the activity with photographs of the pupils making and navigating the mazes. Include the written directions as evidence of understanding.

 Assessment methods: Observe the pupils' individual understanding of the directions and the related vocabulary. Assess with the pupils the written directions to assess understanding.

Addition and subtraction

National Curriculum links

Number – addition and subtraction

- solve problems with addition and subtraction:
  - apply their increasing knowledge of mental and written methods
- add and subtract numbers using concrete objects, pictorial representations, and mentally, including:
  - a two-digit number and ones
  - a two-digit number and tens
  - two two-digit numbers
  - adding three one-digit numbers

Vocabulary	addition, subtraction

Resources	dominoes; clipboard, paper and pencil per group; four gym hoops; prepared problems:
	    5 × two-digit + ones (e.g. 12 + 2),
	    5 × two-digit + tens (e.g. 31 + 20),
	    5 × two-digit + two-digit (e.g. 28 + 11),
	    5 × three one-digit (e.g. 5 + 4 + 8);
	blank sheets of paper; a camera or tablet device

Prior learning	counting in steps of 2, mental maths
Cross-curricular links	Art – creating and observing patterns; PSHE – working as a team

Introduction

Ask pupils to arrange a random collection of 10 dominoes in a line on a table in the classroom, matching the numbers at the ends of the tiles. Ask each pupil to walk along the line of dominoes and add the numbers on the dominoes, using paper and a pencil to record their answers and to help them complete the additions if required.

Hoop problems

Divide pupils into four groups and give each group member some paper and a pencil. Place four gym hoops on the ground and place the prepared problems inside (one hoop for the two-digit numbers and ones; the second hoop for the two-digit numbers and tens; the third hoop for the 2 two-digit numbers, and the fourth hoop for the 3 one-digit numbers).

Assign each group a starting hoop. The pupils have five minutes at each hoop, and should work together to answer the problems and record their answers.

Ask each group to use the blank sheets to create one new problem for each hoop. Check their work and, if there is time, ask the other groups to answer the problems.

 Extension activity: Use the blank sheets of paper to create some subtraction problems for each hoop. There should be 1 two-digit number in each problem (e.g. 30 – 2 – 3 – 4). Ask the groups to revisit each hoop and answer the questions. More questions could be created and answered by the pupils in their groups, using the blank sheets of paper. Challenge the pupils to add up all the answers from each hoop.

 Recording/evidencing: Copy the group answer sheets and stick in each pupil's maths book. Take photographs of the activity or video pupils as they complete the problems in each hoop.

 Assessment methods: Check pupils' answers to the problems to gauge understanding and progression of addition and subtraction. Observe the pupils working out the answers.

Exploring symmetry

National Curriculum links

Geometry – properties of shapes

- identify and describe the properties of 2-D shapes, including the number of sides and line symmetry in a vertical line

Vocabulary	symmetry, lines of symmetry, reflective symmetry, pattern
Resources	a symmetrical object; a piece of paper cut into a shape with a line of symmetry; collection of symmetrical leaves; small rectangular mirrors with no frames; magnifying glasses; three sticks; skipping rope
Prior learning	knowledge of 2-D shapes
Cross-curricular links	Art – making shape pictures; Science – materials

Introduction

Explain the meaning of symmetry: a 2-D shape is symmetrical if a line can be drawn through it so that either side of the line looks exactly the same, but the opposite way around. The line is called a 'line of symmetry'. Use a symmetrical object to model a line of symmetry with a stick.

Model the term 'reflective symmetry' by folding your paper shape along the line of symmetry and showing that each side reflects the other. Explain that there are many examples of symmetrical shapes in nature. Give pupils the leaves, provide some small mirrors, and ask the pupils to see if the leaves are examples of reflective symmetry. They can do this in two ways: by folding the leaves, and also by putting the mirror along the line of symmetry to see if each half-leaf and its reflection still look like the whole leaf.

Naturally symmetrical

Explore the grounds, looking for and naming 2-D shapes in nature and looking for symmetry. Look for shapes in tree trunks, leaves, blades of grass and flowers. Collect some of these natural resources.

Provide the magnifying glasses and the mirrors, and ask pupils to find the lines of symmetry in the natural resources they have found. Ask them to make a list of the items under the headings 'Symmetrical' and 'Non-symmetrical'. Pupils could stick the symmetrical items onto the sheet, or draw pictures of them, and show the line of symmetry.

Split the pupils into three groups and provide each group with a stick. Ask each group to make a picture that has reflective symmetry using natural materials and the stick as the line of symmetry (mirror line), and a second picture that is not symmetrical.

 Extension activity: Using a skipping rope as a line of symmetry, ask the whole class to arrange themselves in a symmetrical pattern on either side of it (e.g. the group could make a pattern of one person standing, one person crouching).

 Recording/evidencing: Stick copies of pupils' lists of symmetrical and non-symmetrical items into their maths books.

 Assessment methods: Check the written lists for correct identification of symmetry. Observe and assess each group's symmetrical pictures, assessing both understanding of symmetry and recognition of the line of symmetry.

Properties of shapes

National Curriculum links

<u>Geometry – properties of shapes</u>

- Year 1: recognise and name common 2-D and 3-D shapes

- Year 2: identify and describe the properties of 2-D shapes, including the number of sides

- Year 2: identify 2-D shapes on the surface of 3-D shapes [for example, a circle on a cylinder, a triangle on a pyramid]

Vocabulary	2-D shapes, triangle, square, rectangle, pentagon, hexagon, 3-D shapes, cube, cuboid, pyramid
Resources	craft matchsticks; reusable adhesive; sticks and poles in various lengths from approximately 10cm to 1m, all no more than 5cm diameter; masking tape; string; scissors; a camera or tablet device
Prior learning	2-D shapes, naming of 3-D shapes
Cross-curricular links	Art – use a range of materials creatively to design and make products

Introduction

Provide each table of pupils with a selection of craft matchsticks and some paper then ask them to create a triangle, a square, a rectangle, a pentagon and a hexagon on the paper. Remind pupils that these are 2-D shapes. Ask them to try to create a cube; how could they hold the shape together?

Sticking around

Divide the class into groups of four or five. Discuss how to use the sticks/poles safely. Define safety boundaries with the pupils (e.g. how to move around with the sticks, make sure they are aware of other pupils at all times).

Ask the groups to create shapes with 3, 4, 5, 6, 7 and 8 sides using the sticks, then ask them to name as many of them as they can.

Challenge the groups to use the sticks to make a large picture containing the most shapes possible. Visit each group's shape picture as a whole class, and name each shape and count the vertices and the sides of each one. Ask the groups to make a shape or picture that includes as many triangles as possible.

 Extension activity: Provide the masking tape and string, and allow pupils to experiment with the sticks to make a 3-D shape. This could be a cube, a cuboid or a pyramid. Can they make a structure large enough to crawl inside, which has triangles as sides? For example, eight sticks will make a square-based pyramid – four sticks at the base to make a 2-D square, then four vertical sticks joined together at the apex. Show pupils how to hold the sticks together with string, rope or tape about 10cm from the top, and then stand them upright, with each stick separated and secured or pushed into the ground to make a tepee shape. Look at the shape of the tepee – is it a pyramid?

 Recording/evidencing: Take photographs of the pupils' shapes and create an online shape guide with the pupils, asking the pupils to label each photo.

 Assessment methods: Observe the pupils and assess their ability to name 2-D shapes and their properties, and their ability to recognise a 2-D shape as a face of a 3-D shape.

National Curriculum links

Statistics

- interpret and construct simple pictograms, tally charts, block diagrams and simple tables
- ask and answer simple questions by counting the number of objects in each category and sorting the categories by quantity
- ask and answer questions about totalling and comparing categorical data

Vocabulary	data, tally chart, pictogram, tables
Resources	a copy of the book *Birdsong* by Ellie Sandall; chalk, paper and pencils; clipboards; garden bird identification guide; optional – bird song app on a tablet device; stopwatch; a camera or tablet device
Prior learning	ask and answer simple questions by counting the number of objects in each category and sorting the categories by quantity; pictograms and tally charts
Cross-curricular links	Science – identify and name animals, gather and record data to help answer questions

Introduction

This is a great activity for spring/early summer.

Ask the pupils if they can name some common garden birds, and if they can demonstrate any bird calls. Have they seen any birds in the school grounds? Look at a bird identification guide together and identify birds they might have seen at school or at home.

Talk to the pupils about why birds sing and how they are using their song to give each other messages (maybe a warning that a large bird or predator is coming, or telling their rivals to keep away from their territory).

Demonstrate how a tally chart works by recording the eye colour of the class members – blue, brown, green, other. Provide pupils with an outline of an eye and help them to make a pictogram using the information from the tally chart.

If using a bird song app, model how it works.

Tally ho!

Take the pupils into the school grounds and ask them to predict which areas would be best for listening to bird song. Help pupils to create a tally chart with a title. Explain that they will need to listen carefully and make a mark on their chart each time they hear any bird song, recording in groups of five. Allow five minutes for this activity.

Read aloud the book *Birdsong* and ask the pupils to mimic the calls they have heard. If using a bird song app, see if any particular bird species can be identified. Look at pictures of birds in the bird identification guide.

Ask the pupils to make new tally charts, this time with the names of individual birds if a bird song app is being used. If a bird song app is not being used, sit as a group for three to five minutes and listen carefully for any different bird song. Together, describe the bird songs heard and use the words to make tally headings for the next part of the activity (e.g. tweet tweet; rah rah ree).

Ask pupils to listen for five minutes and count and record how many different species can be heard, for example if they hear four pigeon calls, three blackbirds and two robins, they should mark IIII for pigeon, III for blackbird and II for robin. Ask the pupils to listen again and record how many times they hear birds with the same call.

Gather the pupils together with their results. Choose one pupil to give their results for a particular bird species. Discuss whether other pupils have different results, and why that might be.

Draw the outline of a large table on the playground or on a large piece of paper and record the results in a massive pictogram; choose a shape to represent a bird. Provide each pupil with a blank table to complete.

 Extension activity: Draw a block diagram on the playground and record the data gathered but, instead of colouring the sectors in, ask the pupils to draw relevant pictures in the chart.

 Recording/evidencing: Retain each pupil's individual work, and take photos of the pupils drawing the pictogram and bar charts.

 Assessment methods: Assess each pupil's understanding of collecting data onto a tally chart, and their ability to use this data to create a pictogram and bar chart.

National Curriculum links

Measurement

• choose and use appropriate standard units to estimate and measure mass (kg/g); temperature (°C); capacity (litres/ml) to the nearest appropriate unit, using rulers, scales, thermometers and measuring vessels

Vocabulary	mass, capacity, record, estimate, compare, more than, less than, equal to
Resources	2-litre plastic bottles (one per group) with the top cut off and retained, and small holes in the bottles (made with a nail or embroidery needle by adult beforehand); jugs of water and funnels, two bowls and scales (one set per group; basic kitchen scales are adequate); large sack of rice (approx. 10kg); soil; composting ingredients (bulking materials: dead grasses, pieces of cardboard egg boxes, shredded newspaper, small wood chips; microbe materials: weeds, leaves, carrot and apple peelings, lettuce, chopped banana skins, bread crusts, all freshly stored in separate bags); small bottles of water; paper, pencils and clipboards; a camera or tablet device
Prior learning	comparing and describing lengths and heights, capacity and volume; measuring and beginning to record mass/weight and capacity and volume
Cross-curricular links	Science – explore and compare the differences between things that are living, things that have died and things that have never been alive

Introduction

In the classroom, put the pupils into groups and provide each group with a 2-litre bottle, a bowl of rice, some scales and a funnel. Ask them to estimate how much rice will be needed to fill the bottle, and to transfer that much rice to a second bowl. Ask them to transfer the rice into their bottle to see how close their estimate is, and to weigh and record the mass of the rice.

Rot-bots

The pupils will be creating their own 'rot-bots' – filling plastic bottles with natural materials which will, over time, change from their current state into compost or special soil. Take the scales and the resources outside.

Ask pupils to take their bottles and give each group around 50 grams of soil in a container, plus some paper and pencils. In pairs, have pupils explore a defined area of the school grounds and collect dead leaves, grasses and dandelions. Allow 5–10 minutes for this. Point out that they are not to pick living leaves from trees or any other plants. Provide access to the materials in the bags. Look at the composting ingredients and discuss which were from a living thing and which were not.

Ask the pupils to estimate whether they have enough ingredients altogether to fill their bottle. Ask them to weigh their collected ingredients and record their results.

Ask each group to fill their bottle with their collected ingredients. Did they have enough? If they need to collect more materials, then ask them to weigh and record each amount, doing so until the bottle is full. Then ask the pupils again to weigh the filled bottles and record the amounts.

Ask questions such as:

- If we break the material into smaller pieces, can we fit more or less of it inside the bottles?
- What happens if we squash the material inside the bottle?
- Most importantly – is the bottle now really full?

The pupils may assume that the bottle is now full of the collected materials. Ask them to add their 50g of soil. Explain that the soil is smaller and will fill any spaces left by the larger materials.

Ask the pupils to add the 50 grams of soil to their list of ingredients in the bottle. Can the pupils estimate the mass of the ingredients in the bottle?

Ask the pupils again if the bottle is now full. Offer each group a funnel and a measuring jug containing 1 litre of water, and tell the pupils to put the bottle onto a water-resistant surface and pour in enough water to saturate the material in the bottle, making sure the water does not overflow. Ask the pupils to measure the amount of water they add and record this amount.

Ask the pupils to weigh the bottles again and record their results. Ask the pupils to label their bottles and put them in a suitable storage place, and explain that the bottles are now *really* full and that their contents will, over time, turn into compost.

 Extension activity: Compare results: which group has the heaviest bottle – including the contents and the water – and which the lightest? Ask each group to compare the weights, using the language of equal to, more than and less than.

 Recording/evidencing: Use the pupils' written measurements, supplement with photos of their rot-bots and include in their maths books.

 Assessment methods: Assess the pupils' understanding of weighing in grams and recording measurements, and their ability to weigh accurately.

Telling the time

National Curriculum links

Measurement

- Year 1: tell the time to the hour and half past the hour and draw the hands on a clock face to show these times

- Year 2: tell and write the time, including quarter past/to the hour and draw the hands on a clock face to show these times

Vocabulary	quarter to, quarter past, half past, o'clock
Resources	picture of pie, cake or pizza seen from directly above and divided into quarters; teaching analogue clock; one hoop, chalk and a pair of sticks (one a bit longer than the radius of a hoop, the other clearly shorter) per group; a camera or tablet device
Prior learning	fractions: $\frac{1}{4}$ $\frac{1}{2}$ $\frac{3}{4}$
Cross-curricular links	PE – basic movement

Introduction

Look together at a teaching analogue clock and ask the pupils to point to half past and o'clock times and say what time it is using the language of o'clock. Look at a picture of a pie, cake or pizza and ask the pupils to define its halves and quarters. Explain that, on a clock, $\frac{3}{4}$ is $\frac{3}{4}$ past the o'clock but we say it as quarter to because when another quarter is added, it will be the next whole hour.

Hold up a pair of sticks. Explain that when you go outside, the short stick will be like the clock's short hand (the hour hand) and the long stick the long hand (the minute hand).

Making a human clock

Sit the pupils down in a circle. Explain that they are going to make a human clock. Draw a chalk circle inside the pupils and mark the hour numbers, 1–12, on it. Point out the pupil who is nearest each number.

Ask the pupil to stand up who is nearest:

- the hour they start school (probably about 9)

- the hour they start their lunch break (12)

- the hour they go home (3).

Stand in the middle of the 'clock' and point a short stick in turn at the 12 different 'number' pupils you have identified; each of them stands up and sits down again. Then explain that the short stick is like the short hand on a clock, and it shows the hour. Knowing this lets us know roughly what time it is.

Place the short stick on the ground so it is pointing to about $\frac{1}{4}$ of the way between 9 and 10 and ask 'What's the time now?' Elicit that the stick looks nearer 9 o'clock, so the time is approximately 9 o'clock, but we can't tell exactly what time it is. Leave the short stick in place.

Explain that this is where the long stick will help. Each hour, the long stick goes all the way around the clock face once, showing us exactly how far through each hour we are. Place the long stick so it is pointing to quarter past, showing we are at exactly quarter past. Say 'Look at the short stick! We're at quarter past …?' (nine).

Move the short stick to halfway between 9 and 10, and the long stick to half past; check for understanding again. Then move the short stick to $\frac{3}{4}$ of the way between 9 and 10, and the long stick to quarter to; finally, move the short stick to 10 and the long stick to o'clock. Ask the pupils the time now (ten o'clock).

Split the pupils into groups of three or four with their hoops and sticks. Ask them to put their hoop on the ground and mark 1–12 inside the hoop, then **o'clock** outside the 12, $\frac{1}{4}$ **past** outside the 3, $\frac{1}{2}$ **past** outside the 6, and $\frac{1}{4}$ **to** outside the 9.

Call out '3 o'clock' and ask the groups to put their sticks – short stick first – in their hoop to point to the time. Check for correctness. Call out half past three, reminding them to use the short stick first – pointing halfway between the 3 and the 4 – and then the long stick to show half past. Continue calling a range of o'clock, quarter to, quarter past and half past times, making sure pupils always put the short stick down first.

 Extension activity: Ask each group to set their hoop clock to a $\frac{1}{4}$ past, $\frac{1}{2}$ past or $\frac{1}{4}$ to time. Regroup and then, as a class, visit each hoop, asking the other groups to tell the time.

 Recording/evidencing: Take photos of the pupils involved in the activity, and print them for their maths books and teacher records. Annotate each individual pupil's photo with a relevant comment.

 Assessment methods: Assess the pupils' ability to tell the time using o'clock, $\frac{1}{4}$ past, $\frac{1}{2}$ past and $\frac{1}{4}$ to the hour.

National Curriculum links

Number – multiplication and division

- recall and use multiplication and division facts for the 2, 5 and 10 multiplication tables, including recognising odd and even numbers

- calculate mathematical statements for multiplication and division within the multiplication tables, and write them using the multiplication (×), division (÷) and equals (=) signs

- solve problems involving multiplication and division, using materials, arrays, repeated addition, mental methods, and multiplication and division facts, including problems in contexts

Vocabulary	equals, multiply, divide, array
Resources	three tarpaulins or sheets; stones and pebbles; pencils and paper for each group; stopwatch; 60 wooden clothes pegs; a marker pen per group; 30 lolly sticks (15 marked with × and 15 with ÷ in the centre of the stick, and all of them marked with = near its right-hand end, with spaces in between big enough to attach the pegs); a camera or tablet device
Prior learning	2, 5 and 10 multiplication tables
Cross-curricular links	Design – selection of materials

Introduction

Split the class into three groups to represent the 2, the 5 and the 10 multiplication tables. Ask each group to stand in a circle, and ask the pupils to call out the table in order around the circle. When they have finished, give them a different table so that after three rounds each group has had a turn at revising all the multiplication tables.

The missing number

With the class in the same three groups, ask the pupils to collect as many small stones and pebbles as they can from the school grounds. Set out the three tarpaulins or sheets, securing each corner with a large stone or a weight.

Ask each group to write out 10 different problems on their paper: five multiplication and five division problems from 'their' table. Allow five minutes for each group to create these challenge sheets. Check the challenge sheets, then ask the pupils to place their sheet on their tarp.

Tell the pupils they have 20 minutes to visit the stations of the other two groups (10 minutes per station). Each group is to use their pegs and lolly sticks to represent the questions on the sheet. For example, if a question is 4 × 2 = ?, they choose a × lolly stick, then write a number 4 on one peg and attach it to the start of the lolly stick (before the × symbol) and write a number 2 on another peg and attach it to the lolly stick after the × symbol. They then use the correct amount of stones/pebbles to form an array representing the answer.

Once each team has completed the 10 questions, the pupils raise their hands and have their results checked and photographed and their pegs and lolly sticks collected. The challenge sheet remains on the tarp and, when all three groups have finished, each group goes to the next station. They do not need to visit the station they created.

 Extension activity: Once the groups have completed the challenges, the class should stand up in their groups. One group calls out problems related to their multiplication table and the remaining pupils jump the same number of times as the answer. Ensure all groups have a turn.

 Recording/evidencing: Photograph the answers to the problems. The photographs may be printed and stuck into individual work or maths books, and annotated with individual comments.

 Assessment methods: Observe the groups working together in turn and record anything significant including individual participation.

National Curriculum links

Number – addition and subtraction

• add and subtract one-digit and two-digit numbers to 20, including zero

Vocabulary	add, subtract, equals, total
Resources	water guns and pumps of different sizes; chalk; four buckets of mud; water; waterproof clothing and boots; towels; a set of large waterproof numbers, 1–20; optional, eight A1 sheets with target rings 0–20; a camera or tablet device
Prior learning	addition and subtraction, and mental maths
Cross-curricular links	Science – forces

Introduction

On the board, draw a large target with 20 circles, each numbered 1–20, and write 10 addition and subtraction sentences with answers less than 20. Ask the class to call out the answers and put an X in the answer circle on the target.

Discuss the sport of archery and explain to pupils that they will be going outside and playing some archery games. Make sure the pupils have their waterproof clothing and boots on because they will be using water and mud for target practice.

Mud slingin' and water shootin'

Draw a 1–20 target, diameter between 5m and 10m, on the playground, marking the circles with your waterproof numbers. (This can be pre-drawn before the lesson, or you could encourage pupils to help draw the circles.) Also mark out a line for pupils to stand behind. Call out an addition or subtraction problem with an answer less than 20 and ask the pupils to call out the answer. Stand just behind the line and model using the water gun to aim for the correct answer. Set some addition and subtraction problems and allow the pupils to have a go at hitting the correct answer.

Split the pupils into four groups. Ask each group to come up with a name for their team. Draw two targets per group on a wall or fence (or use a permanent marker to draw targets on A1, A2 or A3 sheets of card or laminated paper and hang or stick these to the wall). Each target should include numbers from 0–20; one target with odd numbers, the other one with even numbers. You should have a total of eight targets on the wall.

Mark a line for the groups to stand behind. Assign two groups to a teaching assistant and, together with the assistant, call out an addition or subtraction problem. The pupils take turns to call out the answer before they take aim. With the help of the teaching assistant, observe and record each group's answers. After each member of each team has had a go, the winning team is the one that has the most correct answers.

Use the target drawn on the playground (or draw a second target and split the class into two groups). Provide a bucket of mud. Call out addition and subtraction problems and allow the pupils to take turns at mud-slinging. The pupils should take a tennis ball sized lump of wet mud to sling at the target. Take photos of both activities.

 Extension activity: Split the pupils into two groups. Draw two number lines along the floor with chalk, and mark the numbers from 0–20. Assign an adult to each group, and ask the adult to call out addition and subtraction problems. The pupils take turns to aim the water gun and fire at the right answer.

 Recording/evidencing: Use each team's results sheet and place a copy along with photographs in each pupil's maths book, annotated with individual comments.

 Assessment methods: Observe and assess the pupils' knowledge of adding and subtracting one-digit and two-digit numbers to 20.

National Curriculum links

Measurement

- choose and use appropriate standard units to estimate and measure length/height in any direction (m/cm) to the nearest appropriate unit, using rulers

Vocabulary	centimetre, metre, measure, estimate
Resources	measuring tapes; a variety of measuring tools (e.g. metre sticks, rulers and pieces of string cut to 2-metre lengths); paper, pencils; a camera or tablet device
Prior learning	using rulers to measure in centimetres
Cross-curricular links	Geography – knowledge of local area

Introduction

Provide each table with a measuring tape and ask pupils how many different measurements they can take of their table (e.g. length, width, height). Ask them to record their results on paper.

Explain to the pupils that they will be exploring the school grounds with measuring tools.

Metres of sticks

Split the pupils into groups of four or five. Issue the following challenge: estimate how high and how long a piece of play equipment is, and then measure it with one of the tools. Then choose something else in the school grounds and estimate and measure how high and how wide it is. Discuss possible items for the pupils to measure (e.g. plants, a small tree or a fence) and then ask the pupils to choose which measuring tool to use. Discuss their choice, how to estimate and how to use the tools.

Ask the pupils to write down what they will measure, what they will use to measure it, and their estimation in metres or centimetres. Discuss how the items could be measured without using standard measuring tools. Pupils may suggest using a stick to begin with, then small stones or chalk to mark the position of the stick, then re-using the stick, recording how many times this was done and marking the position and then adding the total to give an answer in 'sticks'.

Ask pupils to measure their chosen items using their chosen measuring tool and to compare their estimate with the actual measurement.

 Extension activity: Ask the pupils to find a nearby tree that they like and to estimate its height. Ask them to walk away from the tree, bending over every few steps and looking through their legs back to the tree. When they can just about see the top of the tree, they should stop and mark the ground where they have stopped. They should then measure the distance from the mark to the tree trunk. Explain that this is roughly the height of the tree.

 Recording/evidencing: Take photographs of the items the pupils have measured, print them and ask the pupils to write on their estimates and measurements.

 Assessment methods: Observe and assess the ability of each individual to measure in metres and centimetres.

National Curriculum links

Number – number and place value

- count in steps of 2, 3, and 5 from 0, and in tens from any number, forward and backward

Number – multiplication and division

- solve problems involving multiplication and division using materials, arrays, repeated addition, mental methods, and multiplication and division facts, including problems in contexts

Geometry – position and direction

- order and arrange combinations of mathematical objects in patterns

Vocabulary	arrays, pattern, investigate
Resources	pine cones, pebbles, leaves, twigs, feathers, flowers; clipboards, pencils; measuring tapes; whistle; stopwatch; chalk; paper, pencils, pre-prepared answer sheets (see activity); a camera or tablet device; a set of laminated task cards, hung in a trail around the school grounds, saying: • How many arrays can you make using 36 pine cones? Now try another number. Now make arrays to show each of the following: 3×4, 2×5, $6 \div 2$. • Make a pattern counting in threes with leaves and pebbles. • Make a pattern counting in twos with twigs and feathers. • Make a number line with groups of collected natural items (e.g. one feather, two pebbles, three flower petals, four sticks, five leaves). • Recreate this pattern and describe the rule (give an example of natural materials arranged in a pattern, e.g. two leaves, three feathers, two leaves, three feathers). • How many twigs can you use to make a twig tower? Arrange the twigs in a pattern to make a tower (e.g. three twigs placed horizontally, three placed vertically). Lay out the trail so that a single teaching assistant can easily monitor two or three stations.
Prior learning	2-D shapes, multiplication, measurements
Cross-curricular links	PSHE – team work

Introduction

Split the class into four groups and give each pupil a pencil and an answer sheet with four headings: 'Table 1', 'Table 2', 'Table 3' and 'Table 4'. In the classroom, set up four tables with the following tasks.

- Table 1 – have a number line from 1–10 set out; pupils write down the even numbers
- Table 2 – have a second number line from 1–10 set out; pupils write down the odd numbers
- Table 3 – have leaves with the numbers 2, 4, 6, … 20 written on; pupils identify which multiplication table the numbers are from
- Table 4 – have leaves with the numbers, 3, 6, 9, 12 written on and scattered randomly on the table; pupils identify which multiplication table the numbers belong to, and write down the correct sequence of the numbers.

Each team starts at a different table. Pupils write the answers under the correct heading on their sheet and then move on to the next table. Allow 10 minutes for this activity and then explain that the pupils are going to do a similar activity outside.

Maths trail challenge

Keep the pupils in their groups, and explain that each group will start at a different station or task. They will have approximately five minutes to complete each task and, when the whistle blows, they need to move on to the next station. Take photographs of each group at each station. When they have completed the task, dismantle their 'answer' ready for the next group to begin work.

After all the groups have completed all the tasks, regroup and look at the photographs of the pupils' work; ask the groups to explain how they arrived at the answers. Discuss why the results may differ.

 Extension activity: Regroup as a class. Send each group to a different station and ask them to create a question. The question must be a multiplication or division question, and have a clear numerical answer. For example – what is 6 × 3? What is 8 divided by 2? Ask the groups to write their questions on paper and leave at the station. Revisit each station and, as a class, call out the answers to the questions.

 Recording/evidencing: Use the individual answer sheets as well as photos of the pupils participating in the activity and the photos of their number lines, arrays and patterns as a record.

 Assessment methods: Observe the discussion taking place at the question locations, both inside and outside of the classroom, and check classroom answer sheets. Look for how effectively the pupils have been using materials, arrays, repeated addition, mental methods, and multiplication and division facts. Assess the pupils' abilities to solve problems using the equipment provided.

Acknowledgements

Published by Keen Kite Books
An imprint of HarperCollins*Publishers Ltd*
The News Building
1 London Bridge Street
London SE1 9GF

ISBN: 9780008238490

First published in 2017

10 9 8 7 6 5 4 3 2 1

Text and design © 2017 Keen Kite Books, an imprint of HarperCollins*Publishers Ltd*

Foreword © Michael Morpurgo 2017

Author: Sam Lovegrove

Series Concept and Commissioning: Shelley Teasdale and Michelle I'Anson
Project Manager: Fiona Watson
Inside Concept Design: Ian Wrigley
Editor: Caroline Petherick
Cover Design: Anthony Godber
Text Design and Layout: QBS Learning
Production: Natalia Rebow

A CIP record of this book is available from the British Library